SMELL THE BOOK

SMELL THE BOOK

The Oral History of

MARTY DiBERGI

with

DAVID ST. HUBBINS
DEREK SMALLS
and NIGEL TUFNEL

Foreword by **DAVID BYRNE**

**SIMON &
SCHUSTER**

London · New York · Amsterdam/Antwerp · Sydney/Melbourne · Toronto · New Delhi

Contents

Foreword

by David Byrne

As a somewhat secret Spinal Tap obsessive who follows the blogs, Reddit accounts, and social media rumors, much of this recent history of Tap is already familiar to me. But it's great to have the truth finally come out and the crazy rumors squashed. We didn't ever really believe they'd forgotten us. Or that the ceramics reportedly signed by St. Hubbins and spotted in a Swindon crafts shop were actually made by the reclusive one and only. Nonsense. Nor did we believe that Smalls thought *The Wicker Man* was a documentary and converted to the Anglican faith in a rural community in Scotland. He's always hated Scotland, so this all seemed a bit much to swallow. More rumors followed—an appearance on TMZ with Tufnel pushing a stroller. (Admittedly, it was revealed that it was filled with ale and not an infant.) The media campaigns must end! We have kept the faith. And now we are being rewarded.

The brilliant insights from Tap have become part of our culture—certainly part of musical culture; how many of us on the road have said "These go to eleven" or "Hello, Cleveland!" while lost in the bowels of some dank venue basement. Like in a Borges (or Phillip K. Dick) story, we wonder if the Gallagher brothers are reading from a script written by Tap. As if all of us who claim to be original and innovative yet are unknown even to ourselves are secretly reading from that illustrious manuscript.

And how great that the band, unlike another I won't mention, put aside their differences and animosities and gave the fans one last concert. And they still have it. The magic is still there . . . as is some of the hair. Look through this book. Here, like it or not (and I, for one, completely concur), is a glimpse, a prophecy, of our future, if we dare to bow down and admit it. Relax and let Tap lead the way.

—DB

SMELL THE BOOK

Introduction

One night in 1966, I wandered into a rock club called the Electric Banana in New York City's Greenwich Village. Don't look for it; it's not there anymore. But what I experienced that night, like a first kiss or a first case of food poisoning, made a lasting impression on me. That night, I heard a band that, for me, redefined the words "rock 'n' roll." I was completely blown away by their stage presence, their raw power—and their punctuality.

That band was Britain's now-legendary Spinal Tap. They have since earned a distinguished place in rock history as one of England's loudest bands. At the time, I never dreamed I would one day get the opportunity to make a documentary—an, if you will, rockumentary—about these musical legends. But in the fall of 1982, I learned that Tap was releasing a new album called *Smell the Glove* and planning what was to be their final tour, to promote the album. The news had me licking my cinematic chops. So I loaded my 16mm camera and set out to make rock and film history. The result was *This Is Spinal Tap*.

Although my film was met with critical praise and well over $100 in box office receipts, the band's three principals—guitarist and vocalist David St. Hubbins, guitarist and vocalist Nigel Tufnel, and bassist and vocalist Derek Smalls—were upset. They stopped speaking to me. They claimed that what I thought was an honest and loving portrait of the band was nothing more than a hatchet job. They felt I had placed way too much emphasis on the tour's mishaps. I was crestfallen.

Still, *This Is Spinal Tap* opened doors for me. After years of struggle, documenting weddings and bar mitzvahs and making commercials for La-Z-Boy recliners and Chuck Wagon dog food, I finally got an opportunity to direct a major motion picture: the sequel to an Academy Award–winning movie that had starred Dustin Hoffman and Meryl Streep. Sadly, *Kramer vs. Kramer vs. Godzilla* was met with a somewhat cool reception, and my career in feature films sank faster than a mobster in cement shoes.

After a long period in the wilderness, lost and broke, I entered the spiritual retreat of his holiness Baba Ram Das Boot and spent my days peacefully meditating and reading *Deadline Hollywood*. One day, after my yogic sound bath, I was sipping a spirulina smoothie and scrolling through TikTok when I came across something extraordinary: a video of two legendary country stars singing their version of Tap's famous anthem to women's derrieres, "Big Bottom."

The video was blowing up on social media. This, I would soon learn, piqued the interest of Hope Faith, the daughter of Spinal Tap's late manager, Ian Faith. She had inherited a contract from her father that called for one more Tap performance. What had for the longest time seemed like a worthless piece of paper now smelled of money. So, fifteen years after having acrimoniously split up, Tap was going to reunite for one last concert in New Orleans.

Call it fate, call it karma, call it an IRS notification informing me that I owed a sizable amount in back taxes—I saw this as a sign. So I decided to temporarily forgo enlightenment in pursuit of a filmic rebirth.

I contacted Hope and offered my services. She welcomed the idea. Still, I was worried about the band. In the decades since the original film's release, I had made several overtures to David, Nigel, and Derek in an effort to put the past behind us. Sadly, these overtures fell on deaf ears—not only because of their continuing animus toward me but because they were all battling hearing loss.

But thanks to the passage of time and significant advances in cochlear-implant technology, the guys agreed to give me a second chance. And I believe that *Spinal Tap II: The End Continues* will be the fitting capstone to my directorial oeuvre.

In addition to once again allowing me to chronicle their musical journey, Nigel, David, and Derek also agreed to collaborate with me on the book you are currently three pages into: the oral history of Spinal Tap. A few months ago, we convened for a conversation at the Village Recorders, the fabled L.A. studio where Fleetwood Mac's *Tusk*, Dr. Dre's *The Chronic*, and Whitney Houston's soundtrack to *The Bodyguard* were recorded. We now add the history of the legendary Spinal Tap to the Village's résumé.

But hey, enough of my preamblin'. Whaddya say? Let's historicalize!

—Marty DiBergi, Los Angeles, 2025

CHAPTER 1

Austerity Squatney

T*he future members of Spinal Tap were born into a postwar England struggling to rebuild itself after the Luftwaffe had reduced much of its capital city to rubble. But from this grim landscape, a revolution was about to emerge. A loud one.*

MARTY DiBERGI: Before we talk about the band and how you guys all found each other and started making music, I want to talk about you as individuals—your backgrounds, where you came from. Let's start with Nigel. Where were you born?

NIGEL TUFNEL: I was born in a section of London's East End, far, far, far east—E10, really—called Squatney.

DAVID ST. HUBBINS: E10. Not Eton. That's something else.

NIGEL: E10. That's a postal code. The Aldgate Pump, which has existed since medieval times, is a place in London that demarcates where the East End begins.

DEREK SMALLS: Or ends, depending on your point of view.

MARTY: And what was life like in the Tufnel home?

NIGEL: It was joyful, I suppose. We lived in Buckland Road first, and my dad had the same job as my granddad.

MARTY: Which was?

NIGEL: They made wind socks.

MARTY: You mean the things at the airports that tell you which way the wind is blowing?

NIGEL: Yeah.

DAVID: Top-line. They were the best wind socks.

NIGEL: Yeah. They were handsewn, as they did things then. My mum was a houseperson, as they called it.

MARTY: Did she wash the socks?

NIGEL: No, but on occasion she darned them.

MARTY: Interesting.

NIGEL: It was quite a happy home. My dad was quite musical. My mum was a singer, but not a professional singer. And my granddad was the first to give me a used guitar, a Harmony Sovereign. It was beaten up a bit, but I was thrilled. I think I was about twelve.

MARTY: Did you have brothers and sisters?

NIGEL: I had a brother.

MARTY: And what happened to him?

NIGEL: Nothing.

MARTY: You put it in past tense and I just assumed that he had passed away.

NIGEL: Oh, no. He's still alive, but we don't talk.

MARTY: There's some bad blood there?

NIGEL: Yes. There's a name for it.

DEREK: Bad blood.

NIGEL: No, another name.

DAVID: Brother-shunting.

MARTY: Do you want to talk a little about what happened that caused you not to talk to each other?

NIGEL: No.

MARTY: Was he an older brother or a younger brother?

NIGEL: I don't remember.

DAVID: I've pressed him on this. He's not going to talk. I vaguely remember his brother.

MARTY: What was his name?

NIGEL: Now you've got me under the gun. It was either Philip . . .

DAVID: Or Kevin . . .

NIGEL: Or Charles.

DAVID: I remember he had a rash. Some kind of strawberry birthmark.

MARTY: But you have no idea what happened to him.

NIGEL: Not off the top of my head.

DEREK: Or any other part of your head.

MARTY: Okay. So, David, where were you born?

DAVID: I was born in the same hospital he was, in Squatney. I lived right 'round the corner.

MARTY: So you lived in the same neighborhood?

NIGEL: I was in Buckland Road, and he was . . .

DAVID: In Can Street.

MARTY: How old were you when you first met each other?

NIGEL: It's hard to remember exactly.

MARTY: Well, I'm assuming that if you can't remember who your brother was, it's probably hard to remember the exact age you were.

NIGEL: But that's a different thing. That's a family thing.

DAVID: He's blocking. And there was—maybe you're not familiar with this in the United States—a plague of unexploded bombs that were being uncovered as they pushed the rubble from World War II aside.

MARTY: From the Blitzkrieg. That must have left everyone traumatized.

NIGEL: Especially in the East End. If you'd go to East India Dock Road, you were seeing rubble still.

MARTY: You're not talking about Barney Rubble from *The Flintstones*.

DAVID: No, I never met him. *Admired* him. Anyway, we heard that there was an unexploded bomb right 'round the corner.

NIGEL: The word got out in our neighborhood.

DAVID: And it was like, "We're having that." So we went over to look at it, and that's the first time I laid eyes on Nigel. We were six.

MARTY: And they were able to defuse that bomb?

DAVID: Well, it turned out it was a water tank.

NIGEL: It was from someone's house or something. It looked enough like a bomb that they brought in the experts. But I saw David, and he saw me, and there was just this moment of . . .

DAVID: "Where are you from?" He says, "I live over here." And I said, "I live over there." And we were pointing almost in the same direction.

NIGEL: But we went to different schools. I was at Bunsell Street Primary School.

DAVID: I was at Sacred Sacrament. My mum was a big Catholic.

MARTY: Religious?

DAVID: No, five foot ten.

MARTY: What was life like in the St. Hubbins home?

DAVID: It was difficult because my parents didn't really care for each other, old Ivor and Ruby. There were a lot of rows. And us kids, we would just kind of flinch and crouch.

MARTY: You had brothers and sisters?

DAVID: One sister.

MARTY: And did you know her name?

DAVID: I do. It's Sheila.

MARTY: And where is Sheila?

DAVID: Sheila's gone to Australia. All women there are called Sheila.

DEREK: It's a common noun there.

DAVID: Yeah. So she figured she'd fit right in.

MARTY: You said there was a lot of fighting between your mom and dad.

DAVID: Constantly.

MARTY: Do you remember what they were fighting about?

NIGEL: Yeah, it had something to do with her putting the mustard in the wrong place on the table.

DAVID: Oh, yeah, the mustard fights were legendary.

NIGEL: I remember the first time going over to David's and there was a row going on. So, a lot of those times, he'd come over to my house, where things were calm.

MARTY: What did your dad do for a living?

DAVID: He ran a luggage-repair shop just outside Squatney.

NIGEL: But most of the time he was out on the road.

DAVID: He had this little van and he would travel around to all of the resort areas, all the coastal resorts. Even though his name was Ivor, he called himself Johnny on the Spot. He would park outside the hotels and he would say to people either coming or going, "I see you have broken your luggage, let's do something about it."

NIGEL: Usually, it was handles. Handles break a lot.

MARTY: And that was a good business, waiting outside hotels hoping that someone would turn up with broken luggage?

DAVID: Not really. I think he just liked getting out of the house and away from Ruby. Eventually, Ruby made it official and got away from him.

MARTY: They got divorced?

DAVID: Yeah.

MARTY: How old were you?

DAVID: Fifteen. Right around the time I started playing with this geezer.

NIGEL: We'd go to the clubs. The Ealing Club and the Marquee. The Flamingo was a famous place. We'd see people play and that would then affect how we played.

DAVID: He had all the records.

MARTY: Like 45s?

NIGEL: Well, they were 78s. Ten-inch records from my granddad and dad.

MARTY: I'm going to dive further into how you guys first started playing together. But before we do that, I want to turn to Derek.

DEREK: You turned well.

MARTY: Yes, I physically turned to you, and now I'm looking at you. Derek, where were you born?

DEREK: And I'm turning to you to answer.

DAVID: Letting the action suit the words.

DEREK: I was born in the West Midlands, out in the countryside.

MARTY: What did your father do?

DEREK: In those days, there was a very good business in sanitizing telephones. People were worried about the germs. Word had gotten out.

MARTY: And germs had gotten out.

DEREK: The germs had gotten out. Chasing the words, really, or vice versa. So my dad, Duff, had a little truck that he'd drive about the countryside—and, later on, in the smaller cities in the West Midlands. His business was called SaniFone. When I was three or four, I started riding with him and learning the trade. So even up to this day, if you had a telephone that needed sanitizing, I could do it.

MARTY: Well, it's interesting, because I guess in those days it was all landlines. Now it's cell phones. Is there still a business to sanitize cell phones?

DEREK: It's interesting you ask. I've often thought that if my dad had lived long enough, he'd have a phone-sanitizing app and be a millionaire.

MARTY: You mean an app in the phone that would allow the phone to sanitize itself?

DEREK: Sanitize itself.

MARTY: Like an internal sanitizer.

DEREK: Exactly.

MARTY: And you said your dad's name was Duff?

DEREK: Correct.

DAVID: Is that short for anything?

DEREK: Duffman.

MARTY: Did you have brothers and sisters?

DEREK: No, only child.

MARTY: What were things like in the Smalls home?

NIGEL: Strained.

MARTY: Your mom and dad didn't get along?

DEREK: No. Rosa was a frustrated singer. When I was four, she left us to join a musical quartet called the Hotten Totties. She was an alto in the Hotten Totties.

MARTY: So that's where you get your deep voice.

DEREK: I imagine so. They were touring much of the year. I rarely saw her.

DAVID: What kind of music did they do?

DEREK: It was sort of ragtime, but forties ragtime. So more rag than time.

MARTY: Did your dad ever get remarried?

DEREK: He never did. He was married to his business. To him it was not just a business, it was a calling. *Literally* a calling.

Now *would be a good time for me to fill you in about my own humble beginnings. I was born Martin Bernardi on March 5, 1947. We lived in a predominantly Italian and Jewish neighborhood in the Bronx.*

My father, Anthony Bernardi, ran a hero shop on Arthur Avenue. My mother, Sylvia, was Jewish and a homemaker with a great singing voice. Growing up, our apartment was filled with the sounds of Ella Fitzgerald, Sarah Vaughan, and Nina Simone. When rock 'n' roll made the scene, my mother embraced it. She loved Buddy Holly, Little Richard, and Chuck Berry. Lawrence Welk gave her migraines.

When I was just seven years old, my parents took me and my sister, Rosalie, to the local Loews movie theater to see Prince Valiant. *From the moment I saw Robert Wagner in his pageboy haircut, I knew what I wanted to be. No, not a gay man with a chain-mail fetish, but a filmmaker.*

Though my father was Italian, I was raised as a Jew, and for my bar mitzvah, my parents got me an 8mm film camera. From that moment on, there was no stopping me. I filmed everything in sight, from a butterfly landing on a flower to my father farting as he fell asleep watching The Ed Sullivan Show. *Since the camera had no sound, you couldn't hear the farts. But trust me, they were not silent, just deadly.*

CHAPTER 2

A Sound Is Born

O*ut of the emptiness: salvation! The early days of the Tufnel–
St. Hubbins musical alliance provided a pathway out of hard-
ship and dead-end lives spent mending wind socks and repairing luggage.
But the pathway was anything but straightforward.*

MARTY: When did you first start making music together?

DAVID: It was around the time that my folks broke up, age
fourteen or maybe fifteen.

NIGEL: He was spending more and more time at my place.

DAVID: He had a guitar with all six strings. I had a four-string
tenor.

NIGEL: We would listen to records for hours. Blues records.
Blind Bubba Cheeks was one. Lonnie Johnson, Alexis Korner,
people like that.

DAVID: Also, domestic skiffle like Lonnie Donegan.

NIGEL: Yes. He was huge. And then we eventually started figuring out things from the records.

DAVID: There was one tune called "Hoot Hoot." That was the only lyric, "Hoot hoot." But the playing was fucking amazing.

MARTY: So when did you guys start doing it officially? Where did you perform first?

NIGEL: In the streets. Outside of a Tube station. You put a hat down or whatever.

MARTY: Did you make any money?

DAVID: Enough to buy a new hat.

NIGEL: If you're lucky.

MARTY: Were you doing your own music?

NIGEL: No, we did mostly covers.

DAVID: Well, all covers.

NIGEL: When I said "mostly," I meant "all."

MARTY: What was your first original song?

DAVID: "All the Way Home."

NIGEL: Yeah. And that has skiffle roots.

MARTY: And when was the first time you were hired to play in a club?

NIGEL: Well, you didn't get paid, but you could go to the clubs. The Half Moon in Putney, places like that. You would just show up. And then it was a string of people playing. It would go on all night.

DAVID: I do recall that at one point, we each had a skiffle band. You were in a group called the Lovely Lads. And I was with the Creatures.

MARTY: So the first official group that you were in was not with each other?

DAVID: There was some other connection. I don't even remember who it was. Was it Coy Devon?

NIGEL: No. There was this chap called Bumby.

DAVID: Bumby, right.

NIGEL: He played . . . It wasn't a real bass, it was a string and a washtub. And you could bend this little broomstick back, and it would be the notes. Bumby could play that.

MARTY: So Bumby was like the glue between you guys.

DEREK: I find that people who play bass are often the glue.

MARTY: So, it was you two and Bumby?

DAVID: Yeah, that was the beginning of the Originals.

MARTY: So the Originals was the three of you. Who else was in the Originals?

NIGEL: Well, Bumby was in it for a little bit, and then he left. He went to Richmond and joined some other group. The important thing was to have a name: the Originals, in our case.

MARTY: And that's a great name, because it seems like you were the first to do what you did.

DAVID: Except that we weren't. There was already a group called the Originals.

NIGEL: Also in the East End.

DAVID: So we changed our name.

MARTY: To what?

DAVID: The New Originals. But then, the original Originals broke up.

MARTY: So did you go back to being the Originals?

DAVID: No, we became the Regulars.

MARTY: Do you remember your first gig as the Regulars?

DAVID: Yeah. It was the Queen's Lips.

NIGEL: It was a pub, basically.

DAVID: But they had a stage.

NIGEL: Yeah. We got two pounds or something.

MARTY: Then, from there, I understand, you were hired to be part of the Johnny Goodshow Revue?

DAVID: Yeah. That was fluky, wasn't it? Johnny Goodshow was not his real name. It was just a stage name. He was quite a man about town.

MARTY: He probably thought if he called himself Goodshow, it would be a way of letting people know they'd be in for a good time. What was his real name?

DAVID: Billy Goodshow.

NIGEL: He was a hustler.

MARTY: And you did a tour with him?

DAVID: Yeah. We played the seaside circuit. I knew all those venues from my dad.

MARTY: From fixing the handles on suitcases.

DAVID: Yeah.

NIGEL: I remember Blackpool the best, because there was the deepest sadness about that place.

DAVID: There was one club, the Waves. It was actually a ballroom from the days when they would have dancing and all that. We played this immense ballroom to an audience of about ten.

MARTY: That *is* sad.

DAVID: Then we played in a pub near the Waves called the Bucket. Which is still there. It's now called the Bucket and Pail.

MARTY: That seems redundant.

DAVID: I guess you could say that.

DEREK: He just did.

DAVID: Anyway, that's when we first met Stumpy Pepys.

NIGEL: Yeah, for the first time.

DAVID: That's what I said.

NIGEL: I said it, too.

DAVID: At that time, Stumpy was drumming for the Leslie Cheswick Soul Explosion.

NIGEL: He was good, Stumpy was.

DAVID: Great drummer.

MARTY: How did he get the name Stumpy?

DAVID: I don't know. I've never seen him naked, so who knows?

NIGEL: I was afraid to ask, frankly, because I thought it was you-know-what.

DAVID: You were afraid that if you said, "Why do they call you Stumpy?" he'd say, "Well, it's because of little stumpy here." Anyway, Stumpy joined us, and since Bumby had left music to become an ornithologist, it was only the three of us. Until we found a bass player named Ronnie Pudding.

DAVID: He was with a group called Cheap Dates.

NIGEL: Ronnie was a good songwriter.

DAVID: And he could arrange things. He did the string arrangement for "Rainy Day Sun."

NIGEL: Very talented.

MARTY: And at that point you called yourselves what?

DAVID: The Thamesmen. We did "Gimme Some Money" and we got some traction with it. It actually got played a bit. When we first heard it on the radio, it was kind of amazing.

NIGEL: At first, we thought there was something wrong with the radio.

DAVID: So Nigel hit it.

NIGEL: But our song kept playing, so . . .

MARTY: Is that when you left England?

DAVID: Yeah. We toured the Benelux nations.

NIGEL: Someone knew someone. It's always that. Someone would say, "I know someone in Amsterdam or Bruges or someplace, and you should go there." And we would just pack up and go.

MARTY: And how long were you in Amsterdam?

DAVID: Three weeks. We played a lot of gigs.

NIGEL: The Belgian people loved us. And there were some nice female people in Belgium as well.

DAVID: There still might be.

NIGEL: True. But they're probably dead.

MARTY: And that's when you picked up a keyboard player?

DAVID: Jan Van Der Kvelk.

NIGEL: Yeah. He had one of those funny symbols over one of the letters.

DAVID: Yeah. What are those?

NIGEL: They're not umlauts. They're something else.

DAVID: Omelets.

NIGEL: He was a magical player.

MARTY: It seems like you had a good run in the Benelux nations. But when you left, you didn't take Van Der Kvelk?

DAVID: No, we did. That's when we started calling ourselves the Dutchmen. Because of Jan being Dutch and all. But he didn't stay long because "Gimme Some Money" started charting again. So we switched back to the Thamesmen. But then that faded. And we were kind of at sea.

NIGEL: Not literally.

DAVID: No, not in a boat or anything.

MARTY: You were lost.

DAVID: You could say that.

DEREK: He just did.

MARTY: At this point, you went through a lot of changes. I'm looking at your history. It says that you performed as the Rave Breakers, Hellcats, Flamin' Daemons, Shiners, Mondos, the Doppel Gang, the Peoples, Loose Lips, Waffles, Hot Waffles, Silver Service, the Mud Below, and the Tufnel–St. Hubbins Group.

NIGEL: But it didn't fool the people.

MARTY: Because it was always the same people with different names?

DAVID: Right. But when we became the Tufnel–St. Hubbins Group, that was really sort of a turning point. We started piling on the instruments. Denny Upham and Dickie Lane joined the group. We added horns, Jimmy Adams and Geoff Clovington. And had two female backup singers.

NIGEL: Lhasa Apso . . .

DAVID: And Julie Scrubbs-Martin. Lhasa was my first serious girlfriend. Beautiful girl. She had an adorable lateral lisp. But now we had, like, nine people on the stage. And it wasn't really working the way we thought it would.

MARTY: Was that when you connected with that record executive?

NIGEL: Well, he wasn't a record executive at the time. He was a harp player, harmonica player. Little Danny Schindler.

DAVID: He played with the Schvegman-Hayman-Kvelkman Blues Band.

NIGEL: He was what, four seven?

DAVID: Dripping wet.

MARTY: Well, that wouldn't affect his height.

DAVID: Not technically, no.

NIGEL: He was quite a good harp player. But he was so short. They didn't make microphone stands at that time that could go that low. So for a while, we were calling him Boxy, because he had to stand on a box.

DAVID: He was an Orthodox Jew, never played on Saturday.

NIGEL: Yeah. When he played he'd tuck his payos under his hat.

DAVID: And when he signed with CPR Records, his group was called Talmud.

MARTY: He was really leaning into his Jewishness.

NIGEL: He played klezmer for many years.

DAVID: Heavy klezmer.

NIGEL: Electrified klezmer.

DEREK: Wasn't he known then as Davening Danny Schindler?

DAVID: It was Davenin' Danny Schindler, with an apostrophe.

NIGEL: And on one of the album covers, the picture was him as David, the famous David from the Bible, with that sling thing.

DEREK: And he had the harmonica at the end of the sling.

MARTY: He was going to hit Goliath with the harmonica?

DEREK: It was implied.

NIGEL: It was a famous album cover.

You're probably wondering, or maybe you weren't, where I was developmentally at this point.

My first film was an eight-minute short called Make-Out at the Feast. It was about two teenagers, played by my sister and her boyfriend, who get caught making out behind a statue of the Virgin Mary during the Feast of San Gennaro. Because it included a flash of my sister's breast, showings of the film became a staple at neighborhood parties.

After graduating from Evander Childs High School, I applied to the film schools at NYU, USC, and UCLA. I submitted Make-Out at the Feast as a calling card. Unfortunately, they, along with fourteen other colleges, rejected me. I did, however, get accepted into the Ed Wood School of Cinematic Arts. There I came under the tutelage of Mr. Ed Wood himself, the master filmmaker behind Plan 9 from Outer Space. It was from Mr. Wood that I learned how to dangle a miniature flying saucer on a string to create the illusion of a spacecraft hurtling through the cosmos. Although I never found the opportunity to use this technique in my future filmic endeavors, it served me well as a life lesson. Whenever I was feeling that my directorial career was hanging by a thread, somewhere in the nether regions of my brain I knew I could still fly. And fly I did. Into the waiting arms of Spinal Tap.

CHAPTER 3

The Flowering of Tap

As the mid-sixties dawned, so, too, did a new consciousness among young people. For David St. Hubbins and Nigel Tufnel, the mid-sixties also dawned, but consciousness? Not so much. However, their bassist, Ronnie Pudding, came up with "(Listen to the) Flower People," a song that reflected the times, a song with its finger on the zeitgeist, a song that would forever change the trajectory of the band newly renamed Spinal Tap. And it was with Ronnie's abrupt departure from Tap that a new bassist entered the picture: one Derek Smalls.

MARTY: The first gig you played as Spinal Tap was at—

DAVID: At the Music Membrane.

NIGEL: It was near Leicester Square.

MARTY: Were you playing at the time what has come to be known as heavy metal?

DAVID: We sort of were, but then all of a sudden, everyone was talking about San Francisco.

MARTY: You mean like Scott McKenzie singing, "If you're going to San Francisco, be sure to wear some flowers in your hair"?

DAVID: Yeah, and there were also the Flower Pot Men and all these other groups. So we said, "Let's see if we can throw something together." So we came up with "(Listen to the) Flower People."

MARTY: So your first big hit wasn't heavy metal?

DAVID: Right. We were tempted *not* to call ourselves Spinal Tap.

MARTY: Because the idea of a spinal tap, which is an invasive medical procedure, is kind of at odds with this idea of flower power.

DEREK: A spinal tap is painful, that's really what you're saying.

MARTY: I am saying that.

DEREK: Flowers aren't painful.

MARTY: Not if used properly.

DAVID: Well, stick a rose in somebody's eye, that's going to hurt.

MARTY: So Ronnie Pudding recorded "Flower People" with you. But then he wasn't with the band when the song hit.

DAVID: Right, he was a bit of an egomaniac. He had written quite a bit of "Flower People." We all helped, but he did the most. And his head became enormous. We've always been very democratic, but he wanted to be the autocrat.

MARTY: So what happened to him after that?

DAVID: He formed Pudding People.

NIGEL: Which went nowhere.

DAVID: And he put out an album called *I Am the Music*.

NIGEL: And judging from the sales, the public said, "No, you aren't."

DAVID: So when Mr. Pudding was relegated to the back of the fridge, we met our current bass player. Our final bass player: Mr. Derek Smalls.

DEREK: Thank you very much.

MARTY: And what had you been doing up 'til that point?

DEREK: I was in this band called Mileage, which was sort of dance rock. Which wasn't a thing in those days. And then I joined this really pathbreaking group called Skaface, which was the only all-white ska band. Which got us in a lot of trouble.

MARTY: For, like, cultural appropriation?

DEREK: Yeah. The Skaface Riots were fairly notorious, especially in the North of England.

DAVID: We rescued him from that wasp's nest.

MARTY: People resented the fact that you were all-white?

DEREK: Yeah. And I think we did, too, in a way.

MARTY: You resented yourself?

DEREK: Well, I think we wished that one of us was Black.

MARTY: So "Flower People" becomes a hit. And you play the States, with Derek playing when you appeared on *Jamboreebop*.

DEREK: I was finger-syncing Ronnie's part. It wouldn't have been what I played.

DAVID: But you know what he did? When Derek came in, he learned every tune within days. And then, as we went on touring, we'd noticed that he was subtly changing all the older stuff.

DEREK: Making it my own.

DAVID: We thought, "Great, we have a bass player who's actually contributing."

DEREK: I'm a fast study. Same way I learned to sanitize phones, like this. [Snaps fingers.]

MARTY: So you essentially sanitized Ronnie Pudding's tracks.

DAVID: You debugged them.

DEREK: Yeah.

MARTY: I also noticed that when you did "Flower People" on *Jamboreebop* that there was a new drummer.

DAVID: Right, it was Stumpy Joe Childs. The reason we called him Stumpy Joe was—I forget why. Probably the same reason I forget why we called Stumpy Stumpy. The original Stumpy was great, but sadly he passed away shortly before we recorded "Flower People."

MARTY: And it's well known that he died in a bizarre gardening accident.

DAVID: Yeah.

MARTY: Do we have any particulars on that?

NIGEL: I think it's the vagueness that haunts us, because we don't know how it happened.

DEREK: We don't even know what tool he was using.

NIGEL: That's what I mean. If we knew, let's say if it was a spade or a hoe or whatever, it would be worse in some way.

DEREK: But it would be closure.

MARTY: How would that be closure?

NIGEL: Because then you have the full story in your mind. You know what happened. Right now it's "What do you mean, 'bizarre'? What happened?" "Don't really know." So it just lingers on.

DAVID: So sad.

MARTY: So how did you find his successor, Stumpy Joe?

DAVID: He was playing with a group called . . . Wool Cave?

NIGEL: Yeah. They didn't tune up.

DAVID: No.

NIGEL: That was considered to be—they don't use this term now—but you'd say, "Oh, he's a nancy boy if he tunes up." It was basically saying, "That's a poofter thing, to tune up." Which, again, they wouldn't say now. Although I just did say it.

DAVID: Stumpy Joe was the best part of Wool Cave.

NIGEL: Very powerful drummer.

MARTY: And he stayed with you for quite a while. He played on *Brainhammer, Blood to Let, Nerve Damage, Intravenus de Milo.*

DAVID: And he made the first tour of America with us. We played Boston, New York . . .

NIGEL: Boston again.

DAVID: Boston again, then Chicago.

NIGEL: Then Boston.

MARTY: And you were touring with your album *Listen to the Flower People*?

DAVID: In the States, it was called *Spinal Tap Sings "Listen to the Flower People" and Other Favorites.*

MARTY: What were some of the other favorites?

DEREK: There was a song called "Moon Base." I cowrote it with a girl I was with at the time. It was kind of an LSD thing where humans were setting up bases on the moon and playing rock 'n' roll.

DAVID: And there was one tune we had called "The Spelunker." It was about cave exploration.

NIGEL: It was supposed to be a mysterious sort of thing, because when people go down into caves, you're going into darkness.

DEREK: And do you know what changes that people don't think about? Gravity. The deeper you go in a cave, the heavier you are. So it's no place to be when you're on a diet.

MARTY: So it's the opposite of going into space, where you lose gravity.

DEREK: You get to the center of the Earth and you weigh, like, a thousand pounds.

DAVID: Arthur C. Clarke thought that at the center of the Earth, there's a diamond. Fucking lunatic.

DEREK: It's so hot down there. Wouldn't the diamonds melt?

DAVID: It's not hot, it's just stuffy.

NIGEL: In books I've read—*Journey to the Center of the Earth*, *At the Earth's Core* by Edgar Rice Burroughs—they have different people living there.

DEREK: Did he have Tarzan living at the center of the Earth?

NIGEL: No.

MARTY: But Burroughs was suggesting that there were people living at the center of the Earth?

NIGEL: Yes.

MARTY: Do you think there are?

NIGEL: I don't know, I've never been there.

DEREK: There are no people living at the center of the Earth.

NIGEL: And you've been there, I suppose?

DEREK: No. But why would they be living there? When they could be living anywhere.

NIGEL: Maybe they're not aware of their options.

MARTY: I don't know if we're going to solve this today.

DAVID: Yeah.

MARTY: Tell me about your producer at that time, Glyn Hampton-Cross.

NIGEL: He was a very gifted guy. He could hear parts that we couldn't hear.

DAVID: He had the strangest habit. Sometimes he would start speaking to you like, "Th— sc— crt." I'd say, "What are you doing?" And he said, "I'm leaving out the vowels."

MARTY: He would talk without using vowels?

DAVID: Yeah. So, in saying, like, "Where did I leave the car?" he'd say, "Wh— d— th— cr?" I don't know why he would do it.

NIGEL: He was a prodigy. He went to the Royal Academy of Music and he did the same thing with music. If he was singing a song, he would skip notes. He was so fast that, sometimes, he would skip right to the end.

DAVID: He once sang a piece, all rests.

MARTY: Sounds like a tough record producer to work with, one that doesn't use vowels and skips notes.

DAVID: He had his quirks.

MARTY: It sounds like if he were producing today, he would be into that sound thing where you are close to the microphone and—what's that called?

DAVID: ASMR.

DEREK: What is that?

NIGEL: Is that an assisted-living thing?

MARTY: No, it's like when you, like, rub flannel on five-o'clock shadow very close to the mic.

DAVID: It's supposed to be comforting. I find it annoyingly pointless.

MARTY: So *Flower People* goes gold. Then the follow-up album, *We Are All Flower People*, from what I remember, didn't do as well.

DAVID: We stayed at the dance too long.

NIGEL: It's like that old saying that my granddad used to say, "Ride the horse until he poos." It's that old cliché.

MARTY: Never heard that one.

NIGEL: It's well known.

DAVID: The big problem with *We Are All Flower People* was that Denny Upham, our keyboard player at the time, sort of took over and got very experimental, pulling all this weird crap. There'd be a boogie-woogie riff and he'd reach into the piano where the strings are and start rubbing them.

MARTY: So you fired him?

DAVID: Yeah, we had to let him go. Then we went on as a four-piece for a while, opening for Matchstick Men.

MARTY: And then you finally made a big splash at the Electric Zoo.

DAVID: Right, in North London.

DEREK: Hampstead.

NIGEL: No, it was closer to Islington.

DAVID: Wherever it was, it's not there anymore.

MARTY: And the next album you came out with was *Silent but Deadly*?

DAVID: Yes. We recorded that live at the Zoo.

MARTY: And, Nigel, is that where you started doing your famous solos?

NIGEL: Yeah, that became a signature thing for a bit. People seemed to like it.

DAVID: Until they started to go on a bit too long.

MARTY: What would you say was your longest solo?

NIGEL: Oh, I did ones that were hours long.

MARTY: And you could hold the audience for that long?

NIGEL: No.

DEREK: You didn't hold your fellow band members that long.

NIGEL: No. At a certain point, they'd leave the stage.

MARTY: And do what?

DEREK: I'd usually have a dinner reservation nearby.

DAVID: Sometimes I'd get my waxing done.

NIGEL: So I cut them down a bit.

MARTY: I've noticed that you often incorporate classical elements into your playing.

NIGEL: Well, I didn't study classical music per se—

DEREK: You didn't study it at all.

NIGEL: That's true. It's an unconscious thing. I listen to Beethoven and Mozart, Bach and Corelli. Telemann, Shostakovich, whoever. And it just sort of goes into my head, rumbles about a bit, and then just comes out.

MARTY: So what you're saying is, a healthy diet of classical music keeps you regular.

NIGEL: I don't know what that means, but it sounds right.

I, *too, traveled a long and winding road to artistic fulfillment. Upon my graduation from the Ed Wood School of Cinematic Arts, I was prepared to enter the world of filmmaking. I immediately landed an unpaid job as an assistant production assistant on an industrial film that celebrated the topsy-turvy world of meatpacking. During the shoot, I met the film's producer, Manny Endevers, who was impressed with my ability to deliver six coffees, all with different amounts of cream, sugar, and artificial sweeteners, to individual crew members, always remembering who got what. He said I had a bright future and offered me a lifelong job as production assistant. Although I would remain unpaid, it offered me job security. So I decided to hitch my wagon to Manny and embraced the ever-unpredictable world of industrials. Then one day, while working on a film about coin-operated vibrating beds, it hit me: I was trapped in a career cul-de-sac.*

So I thanked Manny for all he had done for me and bade him farewell. I then proceeded to dust off my 8mm camera and offer up my services to anyone who needed a wedding, a christening, a bar mitzvah, or a bris documented. One day, while shooting Artie Berns's bar mitzvah, I met a wealthy furrier named Murray Gussoff. He asked me if I was interested in directing a commercial for a chain of stores he owned called Murray's Minks. I jumped at the chance. And before I knew it, I became the go-to guy for local-TV spots. I shot commercials for Carmine's Cleaners, Eddie & Freddy "the Bagel Boys," and Salvatore's Pizza Parlor and Shoe Repair, where you could enjoy a slice while waiting for a resole.

I was well on my way to browner pastures.

CHAPTER 4

The World's Loudest Band

The early seventies Spinal Tap lineup—David, Nigel, Derek, and Stumpy Joe—crisscrossed the globe on the backs of Brainhammer, Blood to Let, Nerve Damage, Intravenus DeMilo, and the concept album The Sun Never Sweats, for which they were joined by a new keyboard player, Ross MacLochness.

The endless cycle of album-tour-album-tour was not without its casualties. During the recording of The Sun Never Sweats, Eric "Stumpy Joe" Childs was found dead. To anyone who has seen my documentary This Is Spinal Tap, the story is familiar: Stumpy Joe choked on vomit, but not his own. Because a forensic test for vomit hadn't yet been developed, it wasn't possible to determine whose vomit it was. To this day, the case remains unsolved.

However, I understand that crime labs around the world are developing technologies that shall assist the police and future victims of vomit-choking.

MARTY: Let's talk about *The Sun Never Sweats*. That's when you hired Ross MacLochness.

DAVID: Yes. And having lost Stumpy Joe, Peter "James" Bond came in to play on most of that.

MARTY: How did you find Ross MacLochness?

DAVID: Ross was with a Scottish band, the Kilt Kids.

NIGEL: It was, again, not a great group. They thought, "Oh, we'll dress this way and people will think—"

DAVID: Kilts and tam-o'-shanters. It was what you call in this country a hokey sort of thing.

MARTY: Well, I've seen you, Nigel, dress in kilts.

NIGEL: But that's a real thing. In my family, on my mum's side, she was Scottish. She was a Campbell. That's a real thing. The Kilt Kids were rubbish.

DAVID: They had a mini-opera called *Clytemnestra*. And it had all these vaguely classical references, Greek and Roman.

NIGEL: They had a Greek chorus of sirens.

DAVID: Oh, my God. It was awful.

NIGEL: It was horrible. But Ross was . . .

DEREK: He was a star.

DAVID: A big star.

MARTY: And Peter "James" Bond, how did you find him?

DAVID: He was mostly doing sessions. Yeah, he was a session man.

NIGEL: Occasionally we would do sessions. Not regularly, but I remember I did this thing for some sort of shampoo or dish soap. I was playing guitar and he was there. I thought, "Oh, yeah, he can play."

MARTY: I didn't know you guys played on commercials.

DAVID: I never did. Nigel did.

MARTY: And that's where you met Peter "James" Bond.

DAVID: Peter helped us finish that album. Very heady stuff. And of course, the title track, "The Sun Never Sweats," is Derek's work. A really wonderful piece, but it's a bit demanding.

DEREK: Very demanding.

NIGEL: It's very intensive. And Derek came into his own then, really. He blossomed.

MARTY: What was the inspiration behind "The Sun Never Sweats"?

DEREK: "The sun never sets."

MARTY: The sun never sets?

DEREK: Exactly. That was the inspiration. I said, "Let's put a *w* in it."

MARTY: I see, "sets" became "sweats." It wasn't, like, because the sun—

DEREK: Sweats? No, the sun doesn't sweat.

MARTY: Right. It *causes* sweat.

DAVID: But it's also a reference to the British Empire. "Mad Dogs and Englishmen."

DEREK: It's about the death of English power in the world.

DAVID: Yet it has a very exciting sea-shanty quality to it. It's sort of like, "Yeah, this is all crap and it's all over, thank God. And yet, isn't it fun to play pirates?"

NIGEL: It works on multiple levels.

MARTY: What was the follow-up to *The Sun Never Sweats*?

DAVID: We did another live album called *Jap Habit*. It was actually three LPs and a shirt and a belt buckle, and . . .

DEREK: And a 45.

NIGEL: And a hat, that had that little chin thing. You could fold it and it went right on.

MARTY: Why was the album called *Jap Habit*?

DAVID: We were inspired by our first time in the Far East. We recorded it live.

MARTY: I don't think you could use that title now.

DEREK: We'd get canceled.

DAVID: But the Japanese company that released it, they loved it. They put a fortune into all the gimmickry.

MARTY: And how did that album do?

DAVID: Terribly.

DEREK: It was too expensive.

NIGEL: The Japanese people didn't hold it against us.

DAVID: But Ross was very disappointed. He left the band.

DEREK: He left the music business!

DAVID: He went to Namibia to become a missionary.

MARTY: Really? I didn't know that.

DAVID: Yeah. After he converted what he felt was the requisite number of Africans, he put together an album that he self-recorded.

MARTY: What was it called?

NIGEL: *Doesn't Anybody Here Speak English?*

DAVID: Which did not sell, but it was true to his heart.

DEREK: Well, it was a cri de coeur.

MARTY: A what?

DEREK: You heard me. A cri de coeur. A cri of the coeur.

MARTY: Right, I guess. He was frustrated because nobody there spoke English.

DEREK: Well, they did, it turns out.

MARTY: They did?

NIGEL: They all did. Yeah, he was deluded. It was his excuse for—

MARTY: For failure?

NIGEL: Exactly.

DEREK: He actually got bad reviews in English.

MARTY: So is that when Viv Savage became your keyboard player?

DAVID: Yeah. He was with a group called Aftertaste.

NIGEL: Terrible group. It's funny in thinking now about this, that a lot of the people we found—

DEREK: We rescued.

NIGEL: —were in these rubbish groups, but they were good.

DAVID: Their vocalist, though. The Aftertaste vocalist was Lane something. Something with a *C*. Lane Cartwright?

DEREK: Lane Changing.

DAVID: Right. He could really bring it. He was a really good singer. He had a couple of speech impediments, but a great instrument, as they say.

NIGEL: Yeah, but he couldn't say *w*'s.

DAVID: Yeah, he had a lot of trouble with their version of "What a Wonderful World."

DEREK: He tried to rewrite it.

DAVID: But Aftertaste, they were crap except for Lane. And, of course, Viv, who came over to our side. And he was fine. What he could do, he could play a really strong bass part with his left hand.

NIGEL: He wasn't as dexterous as some of the other people, but he was solid.

DEREK: And he loved to rock 'n' roll.

DAVID: And he looked like a fucking lunatic.

DEREK: Which was a plus.

MARTY: And he joined the band when you recorded *Bent for the Rent*?

DEREK: Not a great title for a record.

DAVID: Not great for sales, either.

MARTY: What does that mean, "bent for the rent"?

DAVID: If the landlord's bugging you and you can't pay them, maybe you'll do them a favor.

MARTY: I see.

DAVID: It's an expression we used to hear around London. You don't hear it much anymore.

MARTY: So the album wasn't successful?

DAVID: No.

DEREK: It stayed well off the charts.

MARTY: And your label at the time was Megaphone?

DAVID: We were with Megaphone for four or five albums.

MARTY: And you sued them over royalties?

DAVID: We sued them because we thought royalties were being withheld.

DEREK: And they sued us back.

MARTY: For what?

DEREK: They alleged "lack of talent."

MARTY: They sued you for lack of talent?

NIGEL: It was quite insulting, really. It said that on the piece of paper.

MARTY: In the lawsuit?

NIGEL: Yeah.

DAVID: And we couldn't prove otherwise, because you can't prove a negative.

MARTY: Did you reach a settlement?

DAVID: Yeah, we agreed to not speak to each other, and we actually had to put it in writing that we would no longer make any product for Megaphone. They were very happy with that.

MARTY: There's a quote I saw from the lawyer for Megaphone that says, "Stay the fuck out of the studio."

DAVID: Yeah, well, that's lawyer-speak.

MARTY: So you don't think he really meant that?

NIGEL: Oh, he meant it.

Like Spinal Tap, my filmmaking career was marked by a mix of highs and lows. In the mid-seventies, one of the local TV spots I did was seen by Dick McGoy, an account executive at a major advertising agency. He asked if I wanted to shoot a series of commercials for Purina's Chuck Wagon dog food. They had this concept of a hungry dog chasing after a miniature checkerboard-patterned covered wagon filled with kibble. I had finally arrived. I could see my feature film career poking up over the horizon. At this point I changed my name to Marty DiBergi as an homage to the great directors I admired: Martin Scorsese, Vittorio De Sica, Ingmar Bergman, and Federico Fellini.

I was on a high. But soon it all came crashing down when the ad company ran out of places for the dog to chase the chuck wagon. The series was discontinued—and with it, my dreams of directing a feature film. I had become typed as the dog-food guy. I was distraught. I had to find a new way in.

CHAPTER 5

The Wilderness Years

The late 1970s was a period of soul-searching for David, Nigel, and Derek, a time for solo projects and early experiments in cave-aging cheese. But Spinal Tap's head-banging days were far from over.

MARTY: Nigel, was there a period where you lived in a castle?

NIGEL: It was a rental in Lichtenstein.

DEREK: Option to buy, right?

NIGEL: Yeah, but not my option. I saw this picture of this castle, so I thought: "Why not Lichtenstein?" And I went there. It's a tiny country. You can drive across it in a half a day. Or half an hour, really.

MARTY: And at that time, you weren't playing as a band.

NIGEL: Not officially.

DAVID: We'd drop in. Occasionally we'd go out and see him.

DEREK: We'd jam with him a bit.

DAVID: We actually started playing around with a concept album inspired by Derek.

MARTY: Really, what was it called?

DEREK: It was called *It's a Smalls World*.

MARTY: Taken from the Disney ride It's a Small World?

DEREK: No, taken from my name. There was nothing Disney about it.

DAVID: You wouldn't want to play that record for children.

NIGEL: I wish I had those tapes.

DAVID: You kept saying, "Let's put this down." And then we'd have lunch and we'd forget.

DEREK: The recording machine was hard to work.

NIGEL: Terribly hard.

DEREK: We never figured it out.

DAVID: You had to have the right change, for one thing.

MARTY: What you are you saying? It was a coin-operated tape machine?

DAVID: Coin-operated, yeah.

MARTY: Nigel, I noticed that when I visited you there, you had some emus.

NIGEL: Yeah. They were there when I got there.

MARTY: Oh, so, they weren't yours.

NIGEL: I didn't personally purchase them. They're lovely creatures, though. A lot of people think, "Oh, they're going to kill me." But emus, they're quite nice.

MARTY: You seemed to be very proud of them.

DAVID: That's called Emu Pride. It's very specific. Some people would be house-proud. He was emu-proud.

NIGEL: People think they would bite you, but they don't bite at all. If they didn't like you, they would kick you.

MARTY: Really? So they're birds that, like ostriches, can't fly.

DAVID: Yeah. A rhea is, too.

MARTY: A rhea is a bird?

DAVID: Yeah.

MARTY: How do you spell that?

DAVID: Like the actress Rhea Perlman.

MARTY: I don't think Rhea Perlman can fly.

DAVID: Never said she could.

MARTY: So after the hiatus in Lichtenstein, you started back up with a new drummer.

DAVID: Peter "James" Bond.

MARTY: And it's been well-documented about what happened to him.

DEREK: Yeah, he exploded.

NIGEL: Onstage.

DAVID: At the Isle of Lucy Jazz-Blues Festival.

NIGEL: Only a little green globule left on his drum seat.

DAVID: Spontaneous human combustion.

DEREK: Which happens much more than you think.

MARTY: Well, it happens a *lot* more than I think. Because I don't think it ever happens.

NIGEL: People don't want to think about it because it's an awful way to go.

MARTY: Can you name other people who have spontaneously combusted?

DEREK: Marie Antoinette.

MARTY: Marie Antoinette was guillotined.

DEREK: Right. But, she exploded first and *then* she was guillotined.

MARTY: Oh.

DEREK: They don't say that part now.

DAVID: You're saying they quashed it.

DEREK: Oh, yeah. Covered it right up.

MARTY: So you're saying that they guillotined an already-exploded person.

DEREK: Makes it much easier, doesn't it?

MARTY: I guess.

NIGEL: If you go and look at Egyptian art, which you see in pyramids, it shows the people, they're all looking in the same direction—

DAVID: They're walking like Egyptians.

NIGEL: —they're looking right or left. And then there's just this . . . *thing*. And that's what that is: an explosion of one of those Egyptian people.

MARTY: Couldn't quite follow that, but—

NIGEL: That's your problem.

DAVID: Did you know that Christopher Lee once went to Paris to watch one of the last uses of the guillotine?

MARTY: That's another thing I was not aware of.

DAVID: Someone said to him, "Would you like to come and see a beheading?" And he said, "Who wouldn't?"

NIGEL: And when he was asked if he wanted to go to a concert called "The Last of the Castrati," he said, "Who wouldn't?"

DAVID: I think he was more interested to see the prep.

DEREK: The auditions, as it were.

NIGEL: They used a lot of mineral oil and—

MARTY: You mean, to turn someone into a castrato?

NIGEL: Which eventually they stopped doing. But they have some recordings of the last of those people. It's a very eerie voice.

DAVID: Can you imagine putting that through Auto-Tune? You'd really hear a whole different story.

MARTY: These people literally are always singing in falsetto.

DEREK: Yeah, like Frankie Valli.

MARTY: Frankie Valli is not a castrato.

DEREK: As far as we know.

DAVID: He *was* on *The Sopranos.*

MARTY: Changing the subject—let's talk about "Nice 'n' Stinky." It came out in the spring of '77 and was . . .

DAVID: A surprise hit, yeah. It was one of those unconstructed things. People heard it on the radio and they said, "There's something missing here." Well, what was missing was pretty much everything except the beat and the feel.

DEREK: We thought people's reaction would be "Where's the content?" But they loved the lack of content.

DAVID: Yeah, we made a choice. In fact, I think if we removed the content out of a lot of our product, we probably would have sold a lot more.

MARTY: Really?

DAVID: Yeah, take it right out. The Spice Girls did it.

MARTY: Interesting.

DEREK: No content, just . . . girls.

MARTY: Yet this becomes a hit, and now all of a sudden you're back together again. But you need another drummer.

DAVID: Yeah. And where did we find him? The Eurovision Song Contest, of all places. The house-band drummer was this bloke, all skin and bones. Six one, dripping wet.

MARTY: Again, you understand that "dripping wet" doesn't refer to height?

DEREK: You get his point.

MARTY: That he was thin.

NIGEL: Yeah, but you could still see him bangin' away.

DAVID: Playing every kind of style.

NIGEL: Anything. He could play anything.

DEREK: For hours!

MARTY: And this is Mick Shrimpton.

DAVID: Mick Shrimpton, yeah. Michael Shrimpton. He had a funny middle name, like Arbuthnot.

NIGEL: It's a Welsh name.

MARTY: So the first record with him was *Shark Sandwich*.

DAVID: Yeah. He really made that work.

MARTY: But it didn't get a great review.

DAVID: It got a lot of bad reviews. Still, it's a very strong album.

MARTY: One of them just said, "Shit sandwich."

DEREK: Let me say this: nobody's reading that review today, and nobody's listening to that record.

DAVID: Perfectly said.

MARTY: This was your first album for Parallel Records.

DAVID: Our only album for Parallel. After *Shark Sandwich* didn't move, they wanted us to change our name.

MARTY: To what?

DAVID: They suggested Popcorn Blizzard.

DEREK: That was one.

DAVID: Underwater Airline.

DEREK: That was another.

NIGEL: We suggested they change *their* name.

DAVID: That didn't go well.

DEREK: They just went out of business.

NIGEL: We went to their office in Soho and they had pad-locked the door.

MARTY: Then you signed with Polymer to record *Smell the Glove.*

And *this is where I climb aboard Spinal Tap's train. Destination: the rock 'n' roll pantheon.*

CHAPTER 6

Faith, Fame, and Festivals

David, Nigel, and Derek were reluctant to talk about their manager, Ian Faith. As devotees of my film are well aware, it was Ian who engineered Tap's return to America for the first time in almost six years, to promote their controversial album Smell the Glove.

When I learned of Tap's pending tour, I thought, This is my chance to return to my documentary roots and free myself from movie purgatory. *I convinced a friend, Mark Spiggler, to pretend to be my agent and call Ian to offer my services. Ian then took my offer to the band.*

I was thrilled when the band agreed. Although the pay wasn't great—there wasn't any—I was certain this would be a marriage made in heaven: a band that I loved and a filmmaking format I cherished. Unfortunately, the marriage met with some nearly irreconcilable differences.

MARTY: Let's talk about Ian Faith.

DAVID: Do we have to?

MARTY: How did he come into your lives?

DEREK: By an evil wind.

DAVID: It was one of those things where we would notice him after a gig. He was always ligging about, you know? We were like, "Who's that bloke?" "I don't know. He was here the other night." And then one night, he comes up to us and says, "You guys are going nowhere, and the reason I know this is because I'm here every night watching you go nowhere."

DEREK: "And I live in nowhere."

DAVID: Well, he didn't say that.

DEREK: No, he didn't say that.

DAVID: He could have.

DEREK: He should have.

DAVID: He convinced us that if we put ourselves in his hands, we would make a go of it, 'cause at the time, we were only occasionally gigging, not recording at all.

DEREK: We were handling ourselves.

DAVID: Sometimes in public.

DAVID: Then he said the two words that are a red flag for you not to trust a person.

MARTY: Which are?

DEREK: "Trust me."

NIGEL: The thing about managers is, it's almost like they're on you before you even know they're there. It's sort of like as if someone farted. You don't see them, you just sense their presence. And then they're there.

MARTY: So what you're saying is, you could smell Ian before you saw him?

NIGEL: Yeah, it's this sense that "Mmm, something's off here."

DAVID: They prey on your self-doubts. If you're thinking, "Maybe there's some reason I'm not making it," the manager senses that and tells you the only reason you're not making it is that you don't have him.

NIGEL: Exactly.

DAVID: And if it happens at exactly the right moment, you're done.

MARTY: And Ian sensed that moment.

DAVID: He did.

DEREK: And he *dealt it.*

DAVID: Silent but deadly.

MARTY: Like your album's title?

DAVID: The phrase has many uses.

DEREK: He kept saying to us, "You have no trajectory. You have no trajectory."

DAVID: Four-syllable word. Very powerful.

DEREK: I didn't know what a trajectory was.

MARTY: Sounds like he played on your vulnerability.

DAVID: Yeah. *He* seemed to be doing really well. We saw him shake down a couple of promoters and it was pretty impressive.

DEREK: Sometimes blood was involved.

DAVID: It's not a nice business.

NIGEL: And he was not a nice man.

DEREK: So we thought he was a good fit.

NIGEL: It's a low calling, really.

DAVID: Sort of like a basso yodeler: a low calling.

MARTY: I see what you're saying. So we're at the point where I come into the picture. You were planning a tour of the United States with the *Smell the Glove* album.

DAVID: And you had seen us in New York.

MARTY: At the Electric Banana.

NIGEL: It was a fun place.

MARTY: And you guys blew me away. Of course, I had been a fan long before *Smell the Glove*, so I was so excited to document the tour. But when the film was finished, I was upset by your reaction.

NIGEL: I remember feeling hurt and feeling betrayed.

MARTY: You felt that I portrayed you in a bad light.

DAVID: You seemed to only focus on the negative stuff, the mishaps.

DEREK: There were dozens of gigs where we found the stage straightaway. We didn't see that reflected.

NIGEL: It was twisted. You could document any group and they have things go wrong—drummers falling off their stools, singers falling off the stage. But they're not shown. If they're not shown, no one knows. And some people were laughing at us.

MARTY: You think I should have shown the times where you successfully found the stage?

DEREK: Why not?

DAVID: Jeanine wasn't so crazy about the way she was portrayed. That made for a rough decade for me.

MARTY: But the film created a rebirth for Tap. You had success in Japan. And later, you came back to the U.S. and did pretty well.

DAVID: Yeah, we started gigging again. We wound up recording another album called *Break Like the Wind*, which came out in '92.

MARTY: Right.

DAVID: And we had a lovely tour. We played the Royal Albert Hall in London. We played Wembley Stadium and Glastonbury.

MARTY: Sounds exciting.

DAVID: It was.

MARTY: But there were stretches when you didn't perform.

DAVID: True.

MARTY: What were you all doing during those hiatuses?

DAVID: I traveled quite a bit with Jeanine, until the money ran out. I studied black magic for a bit in Bavaria. It was only about a week and a half.

MARTY: How much black magic can you learn in a week and a half?

DAVID: About a week and a half's worth.

MARTY: I remember the Live Earth concert.

DAVID: '07, yeah.

MARTY: At that time, you were working at a high-colonic clinic.

DAVID: True. But I was also managing some rap acts. I had one that was fairly successful, big fat Black guy.

MARTY: What was his name?

DAVID: Big Fat Black Guy.

MARTY: Oh, that was his actual—

DAVID: Yeah, and I had a lovely group called Adequit, A-D-E-Q-U-I-T.

MARTY: That seems like a name that would limit their upside.

DAVID: I know. But it came across as modesty. Which is very important in the hip-hop community.

DEREK: They were good enough.

MARTY: And Nigel, when I caught up with you, you were working on a farm that raised miniature horses.

NIGEL: Yes. I became, I suppose, obsessed with miniature horses. They're very sweet and easier to take care of than big horses. You need a smaller area.

DAVID: Smaller paddock.

NIGEL: Yeah. Paddock and stalls and whatever. But I wanted to race them, and I found it difficult to find the little people to race them. The people had to be 2.5 feet high or shorter.

MARTY: And, Derek, when I reconnected with you, you were in rehab.

DEREK: Yes, I was in rehab for internet addiction. I was addicted to the internet.

NIGEL: I remember when I heard about this. I wrote him an email. But he didn't answer.

DEREK: I wasn't allowed. It's terrible. It gets ahold of you, and before you know it, you're looking at cats waterskiing.

MARTY: That's serious.

DEREK: It was. I had to go to rehab twice. That's how bad it was. I thought I was cured, went back home, and—

DAVID: The addiction rebooted on him.

MARTY: I thought it kind of ironic that when I talked to you, we were talking to each other through the computer.

DEREK: Yeah. I was violating my regimen.

MARTY: You also went through a period where you kind of took up where your father left off with SaniFone?

DEREK: Yeah. But, by that time, people had for the most part stopped using landlines. Suddenly there was no money in phone-sanitizing.

DAVID: My dad used to say, "Don't pick your nose. There's no money in it."

MARTY: How does that apply?

DAVID: Who said it did?

In 2009, after playing to huge crowds at the Glastonbury Festival and Wembley Arena, Tap abruptly stopped performing. At the time, no one knew why.

CHAPTER 7

Rockin' in the Urn

I too had disappeared from public view. As I said, I was at the spiritual retreat of Baba Ram Das Boot, looking for meaning, when I learned of Tap's plans to reunite for one final concert in New Orleans in 2024.

When I got the go-ahead to document the concert and work with Tap once again, I was ecstatic. I jumped for joy and sang "Happy Days Are Here Again"—not the slow Barbra Streisand version, but the original up-tempo version by Lou Levin with Leo Reisman and His Orchestra.

The story of how and why the members of Tap became estranged is explained in my new film, Spinal Tap II: The End Continues. Not wanting to be a spoiler-alert guy, I'll disclose that they are playing together again, if only for this one last time. With age, the guys, approaching what some might call wisdom, have grown reflective about the life-affirming powers of heavy rock.

MARTY: We're seeing rockers who started when they were very young—Mick Jagger, Paul McCartney, Elton John, people well into their seventies and eighties—still performing onstage. And it seems like you guys still enjoy playing, too. What motivates you?

DEREK: Rock 'n' roll came out of country music and blues. And those people played 'til they dropped. We're just inheriting that tradition. You play 'til you bloody drop.

DAVID: This might get a bit metaphysical, but rock is built around a beat. Like your heart is built around a beat. When you are young, when you're falling in love for the first time, you're dancing close, you're making out and all this stuff, you're aware of two things: the music and your heartbeat. Well, there's other stuff. But—

DEREK: Three things.

DAVID: Yeah, well, but the point I'm making is, as long as the heart is beating, the rock is there for you. I used to say, "Rock 'n' roll keeps you young, but you have to die young." Now I think, "If you're old, keep rockin' 'til you get older. And then keep rockin' after that."

NIGEL: I think you have to do it. Anyone who's done it early on has to keep doing it if they can. Assuming your hands and voice work, you've got to do it because it's in your heart. Why would you stop if it gives you joy, you know? To play in front of people? People seem to like it. I've been playing in the pub up in the North of England and that's as much fun as anything else.

MARTY: Right. And, Derek, I noticed that you wrote this new song "Rockin' in the Urn," which indicates that even after you die, you still keep rocking.

DEREK: Even death can't stop a rocker from rockin'.

DAVID: Or droppin' *g*'s and addin' apostrophes.

NIGEL: It might slow you down a bit, death.

DEREK: And dampen the tempo.

DAVID: But if there's music in your soul, when you die the music would have to go somewhere, wouldn't it?

NIGEL: That's just logic, isn't it?

DEREK: That's why when I'm ashes, I'll still be bashing.

DAVID: Right. Nothing changes.

DEREK: Just the venue and the makeup of the crowd.

NIGEL: Yeah, and the merch.

MARTY: I want to thank you all for taking the time to talk with me.

DAVID: Sometimes a pleasure, Marty.

Acknowledgments

Marty DiBergi

Where to begin? First, I want to thank my three musical heroes: David St. Hubbins, Nigel Tufnel, and Derek Smalls. Without the trust and support of these luminescent rock gods, this humble purveyor of movie magic would be slicing mortadella at his father's deli. So thank you, gents, for the gift you have given to me and your legions of fans.

To the entire crew of both *Tap* films: Your dedication to helping me capture Spinal Tap's talent and humanity—at minimum wage, no less—has made my filmmaking experience an absolute joy.

To my parents, thank you for believing that a boy with no obvious disadvantages could almost make a living doing what others have been much more successful at.

Finally, I would be remiss if I didn't pay tribute to all the Spinal Tap drummers who have met with untimely endings. To John "Stumpy" Pepys (bizarre gardening accident); Eric "Stumpy Joe" Childs (choked on vomit—someone else's); Peter "James" Bond (spontaneously combusted onstage); Mick Shrimpton (ditto); Joe "Mama" Besser (cause unknown); Richard "Ric" Shrimpton (sold his dialysis machine for drugs; presumed dead); and Scott "Skippy" Skuffleton (prolonged sneezing fit)—may you all rest in peace. And to Tap's most recent drummer, Didi Crockett—all I can say is you knew what you were getting into.

David St. Hubbins

To the women in my life . . . Mum, of course, but also:

Lhasa, Cleo, Diane K., Diane M., Paulette, Lynda, Gayle, Gayle Jr., Liz, Popsy, the girl at the clinic, Hedda, Edie, Deb (fake heiress), Deb (fake deb), Xuxi, Lala, Kelly from Interpol, Muireann (pronounced "Maryann"), Julia (pronounced "Hulia"), Kristen, Kristin, Kirsten, Chicago Red, Caoimhe (pronounced "Kweevah"), the Capricorn waitress, Beige Betty, Ramona, Winter Green, Ynes, Skye . . . and Jeanine.

Nigel Tufnel

First, without Enid and Ollie, my mum and dad, I wouldn't be here. At least that's what my granddad Bertie told me. I think often about how lovely they were.

It was my good fortune to find music. Thanks to all my heroes, especially Blind Bubba Cheeks. His genius was my inspiration.

I must thank my dear Moira for being by my side through the good and bad times.

Finally, to my oldest friend, David, you are, and always will be, in my heart.

Derek Smalls

I would be remissful to not acknowledge my parents, Duffman "Duff" Smalls and Rosa Springer Smalls. He was a wonderful example of how sanitizing people's telephones could be not only a job but also a calling. And she, during the four years I knew her before she decamped to join the Hotten Totties, kindled the flame of music that has never since been extinguished. Or, if it has, I haven't noticed.

My huge thanks to David and Nigel for rescuing me from Britain's only all-white ska band, Skaface. It was a bad idea gone wrong. Dave and Nige, I mean it from my heart's bottom when I say that, despite our differences, we will always have our differences.

My thanks to the lads in the Christian rock band Lambsblood for briefly accepting me into their ranks, despite my reputation for devil worship.

And finally, thanks to the fans, especially those who, every night, gathered backstage for some post-show big-bottomology.